Marriage From
God's Perspective

By Robb Thompson

Marriage From God's Perspective
ISBN 1-889723-18-5
Copyright © 2000 by Robb Thompson
Family Harvest Church
18500 92nd Ave.
Tinley Park, Illinois 60477

Editorial Consultant: Cynthia Hansen
Text Design: Lisa Simpson

DEDICATION

I dedicate this book
to all those who desire to live
in the covenant of marriage *God's* way.
May His way of loving come alive in you.

TABLE OF CONTENTS

INTRODUCTION

Here's a novel idea — let's discuss marriage from a biblical perspective!

Why is that idea so novel? Well, sad to say, but most couples these days aren't looking for a biblical perspective on marriage. They'd rather look for a place of marital compromise. So they go searching for answers to all the wrong questions — questions such as: "Where can we compromise in our relationship in order for us to live together? What am I willing to give to you? More importantly, what are you willing to give to *me*?"

The attitude operating within this type of marriage is "I'm not going to do what I said I would do if you don't do what you said *you* would do!" Many couples end up living in this sad place of compromise their entire married lives.

You can find all kinds of different perspectives in the world today about what it takes to have a successful marriage, but most of what is said about the covenant of marriage is nothing more than man's opinion. Nevertheless, these opinions find a ready audience because so many people are trapped in bad marriages. They're looking for whatever promises them a happy marriage at the least cost to themselves.

Over the years, I've found that the quality of so many modern marriages is poor because the value placed on marriage in these modern times is so low. For instance, some people think it's valid to ask the question, "If a person's spouse should ever become disabled, is it all right for that person to divorce him or her?"

People who ask that question should take a look at the case of "Superman" actor Christopher Reeves and his wife. After a horse riding accident left Christopher paralyzed from the neck down, his wife was heard to say, "Look, I may have married Superman, but to me, Christopher is *still* my superman!" For couples like the

Reeves, marriage is a lifetime commitment, no matter what adversity they may encounter along the way!

I don't know about you, but before I was saved, I was one of those who had a poor view of marriage. As a matter of fact, I saw it as something you could just throw away. If you didn't like the spouse you had, you could just get a divorce and find another one!

Many people have that view of marriage — even in the Church. They care more about looking respectable than they do about honoring their marriage vows. For instance, I once heard of a woman, a member of a large denominational church, who decided she wanted an annulment after being married fifteen years. She and her husband already had five children. But when her husband decided he didn't want to have any more children, she decided to file for annulment.

In this woman's denomination, annulment is more respectable than divorce, and respectability was all she really cared about. She didn't care about what was right or wrong. She wasn't willing to try to make right whatever was wrong in her marriage. She just wanted to start over again, hoping that the second, third, or fourth time around wouldn't be as difficult as the first time. She placed no value on the covenant of marriage.

That's too often the case in Christian marriages today. That's why I believe the Body of Christ is about to go through a real upheaval in the arena of marriage if believers don't wake up and find out what God says about this divinely ordained institution. Right now the Church is about even with the world in the percentage of marriages that end in divorce. But I believe the Church could even surpass the world in this arena if more ministers don't start giving believers biblical answers for their marriages. This lack of strong, scriptural teaching on marriage must be corrected, or the number of Christian marriages ending in divorce will only increase.

When people don't understand God's perspective on marriage, they get married out of the will of God for all the wrong reasons. They marry to rebel against their parents. They marry to get out of their parents' house. They marry because they have believed a lie. They marry because they learned about "love" in the back of a Dodge car.

People also make the mistake of marrying to become complete — to get something they don't have within themselves. But in reality, it is when two people learn how to *complement* one another, like a hand fitting into a glove, that a marriage becomes what God intended for it to be. This kind of marriage doesn't come about automatically. It is achieved when both marriage partners maintain a sense of compassion for one another and practice forgiving and overlooking each other's faults on a daily basis.

You see, two people who decide to get married have only seen each other in certain aspects of life. Before the wedding, they thought, *We enjoy each other's company so much! I don't know how I could live an hour without her [or him]!* But after the wedding, they find out they have to brush their teeth together. She discovers what he looks like before he shaves. He wakes up to the fact that she doesn't look picture perfect when she gets out of bed.

One thing she loved about him during the courtship was that he never really wanted to watch television; he was only interested in her. Now she finds out that he never did quit watching television; he just did it when he wasn't with her. And now that they live in the same house, he's sitting in front of the television for hours every evening!

As the days go by, the relationship doesn't seem quite as illustrious as it did before the wedding day. Marital bliss isn't "shining ever brighter unto the perfect day." The spark begins to dwindle. As time goes by and things get worse, one or both partners may even get involved in an extramarital affair as they look for a way to renew the excitement — the spark — that made them want to get married in the first place.

Sound familiar? Well, let me assure you, my friend, marriage doesn't have to be this way! There is a way to maintain that initial spark in your marriage year after year as it changes both you and your partner into new people!

There is a way you can come to a place in your marriage where you can hardly wait to enter deeper into your relationship with your spouse. There is a way you can grow in love day after day after day. But this goal is achieved by *choice*, not by *chance*. Whether or not your marriage is successful depends largely on each partner's willingness to discover and meet the other person's needs.

But what *are* those basic human needs that both you and your spouse must meet if your marriage is to be successful? Let's find out as we talk about marriage from *God's* perspective. It's time to get on the path toward making your marriage all God designed it to be!

Robb Thompson

Chapter 1

GOD'S DESIGN FOR MARRIAGE

Contrary to popular opinion, when you get married, you don't automatically live happily ever after.

Now, that doesn't mean people should shy away from getting married. Marriage was the first institution God ever established, and He designed it to be a thing of beauty and fulfillment. But although marriage can be the most glorious experience a person ever gets himself into, it can also be the most horrendous!

When your marriage hits one of those "horrendous" spots, you can be tempted to think, *Were we even meant to get married in the first place? Maybe we're wrong for each other.* But the question of whether you and your spouse are right or wrong for each other isn't dependent on the compatibility test you took before you said your wedding vows. It's dependent on how willing you both are to meet each other's needs on a daily basis *after* the wedding.

You see, whether male or female, we all have a deep, inner desire within ourselves to keep covenant. God designed us to be covenant people by nature. At the very core of ourselves, we tend to be religious, seeking for a Higher Power to keep covenant with. As our search leads us to the one true God, the Word provides us with covenant principles that then guide our lives.

Thus, couples who have great marriages are the ones who have learned how to operate in love according to their covenant commitment to each other. They have spent the time necessary to develop a giving-and-receiving relationship. They continually speak God's Word over their marriage and have learned how to be ever ready to believe the best of their spouse.

No person has a great marriage if he or she is a taker. Nor does a person have a great marriage if he or she is always the giver. A successful marriage requires both partners giving to and receiving from one another so their needs can be met and they can enjoy life together.

Mankind's First Marriage

God created everything in this natural realm, including man, and saw that it was good. Then He took woman out of man, and the covenant of marriage was instituted. *"And Adam said: 'This is now bone of my bones and flesh of my flesh; she shall be called Woman* [Hebrew, "isha"], *because she was taken out of Man* [Hebrew, "Ish"]'" (Gen. 2:23).

So if you're a man, take heed: You'll never really perfectly understand your wife because the very qualities she has inside of her are the qualities you are lacking! They were taken out of man's side long ago and placed within the woman. Now in marriage, those qualities are returned to you in the form of your wife.

17

Your wife is to be your complementer and your helper, called alongside you to be someone no one else could ever be in your life. She is to be someone you can trust, someone who will never degrade you or talk down to you. But she is *not* to be another mother to you.

Sure, your mom can cook. Sure, your mom can clean. Sure, your mom can wash your clothes and make everything great for you. But if you were just looking for another mother to take care of you, you never should have gotten married in the first place! Your wife is to be someone in your life you care for — *not* someone you expect to take care of you!

You see, a man has within himself the need to take care of and protect someone. But when bad attitudes develop in a marriage relationship, he may decide he no longer wants to look after and care for his wife. His temptation at that point is to start looking for someone new he can look after and care for. But there is a way to prevent that from ever happening, and it starts when both marriage partners determine to meet each other's needs as never before.

In the beginning, God created a perfect world. The first man and woman were together on an absolutely deserted planet. They walked naked and unashamed with one another in the Garden that had been divinely prepared for them.

Then came that dreadful day when man no longer communicated with his wife. He didn't converse with her. He didn't protect her when the enemy came to deceive. As a result, the woman was vulnerable when Satan spoke to her. She talked to the serpent because she wanted someone to talk to. She told him what she knew, even embellishing what she knew a little bit just to impress him. At that point, Satan knew he had her and began to lure her away from her relationship with her husband and with her God.

Suddenly, the bliss, wonder, and amazement Adam and his woman had continually experienced in their perfect world turned to horror. Genesis 3:8-13 tells us what happened next.

God walked in the Garden in the cool of the day and called out, "Adam, where are you?" There was no reply.

God called out again, "Adam, where are you?" Adam reluctantly came out from behind a tree wearing fig leaves he had sown together to make a covering for himself.

"Adam, where have you been?" God asked.

Adam replied, "Well, when I heard You walking in the Garden in the cool of the day, I was afraid because I was naked."

"Who told you that you were naked?"

At this moment, the blame game began — a game men and women continue to play to this day. "It was the woman You gave me who blew it," Adam said.

"No, it was the serpent's fault!" the woman protested.

In the end, everyone involved was a loser (vv. 14-19). After yielding to Satan's temptation to disobey God, Adam and his wife sewed fig leaves together and made coverings for their bodies. In other words, they not only hid from God, but they also hid from one another. They were no longer interested in one another. They no longer wanted to spend time together. At that point in their lives, all the communication lines were down.

The woman was no longer called "Isha," or "Woman," queen of God's creation. Instead, her name became "Eve" — in essence, "the mother of my kids" (v. 20). God's perspective of a perfect marriage had died along with the innocence of Adam and Eve. The very thing God had meant for good had now turned sour. Only through the redemptive work of a Savior could His original intent for marriage be restored.

We're All Learning

God had given woman to man because He knew it wasn't good for man to be alone. It wasn't good for a man to hide away in his house and never communicate with anyone all day long. Man needed woman to be his helper — someone who complemented him, someone whom he could protect, take care of, and give to.

You know, it's very easy for most men to be alone because they're not skilled at communicating. That's certainly true of me. When my wife Linda and I invite guests to our home for a party, I can often be found off in some corner by myself. The truth is, I'm not a great communicator on a personal level because I take for granted that other people know what I know. But Linda helps me with that weakness. She's my complementer!

All of us have weaknesses and short-comings. We're all on the escalator of learning because none of us grew up perfect.

That's important to remember when you're studying the Bible on the subject of marriage. God's Word presents His perspective on marriage — the perfect way He designed marriage to be. So you have to be careful not to get discouraged and give up when you take your eyes out of the Word and look at the way your marriage really is. Sure, your spouse may have weaknesses and problems, but where are you going to find someone who doesn't?

I'm sure that Linda sometimes thinks I'm hypocritical because I don't always do the very things I teach others to do. But the truth is, although I have a gift to *teach* God's Word, I don't have a gift to *live* it. I have to learn to apply it to my life just like you do. Therefore, although I know I have faults, I refuse to camp around them. I just work on getting better at doing the Word!

We all need to be changed by *doing* the Word, not just by *hearing* it. Otherwise, the truth we find in God's Word doesn't do us any good.

No one is perfect — including you! Jesus knew that, so He didn't die with the intent of leaving us and our faulty opinions in charge of this earth. He died so *His Word* might rule in our lives.

Therefore, it isn't what we think about marriage that counts; it's what *God* thinks about it. We can find all sorts of opinions in the world about what marriage should be. But God's Word gives us absolutes regarding the marriage relationship that will play out with some variation in all our lives. As we apply His eternal principles to our marriages, we'll see how He can take two people with individual weaknesses and make them a testimony of love, faithfulness, and fulfillment to the world!

The Divine Purpose For Marriage

When we expect our spouse to become something to us that only Jesus can become, we put our marriage in jeopardy. Too often we expect our mate to be our savior, our lover, our friend, our helper, and the hardest worker in supporting what we do. But one person can't play all those roles, and we shouldn't expect our spouse to do it.

When I got married, I wasn't looking for a business partner. I didn't marry Linda because I knew she was such a hard worker, although she *is* the hardest worker I know. I didn't think, *Well, it's easier to marry her than to pay her!* I also didn't marry her because I needed a new mother. I married Linda for the purpose *God* designed marriage to fulfill in the first place.

What is that purpose? We get married because there is one who has been called by God to come alongside and be something to us that no one else in life could ever be. We get married so we can finally become naked, open, and *real* before the one we love on many different levels — emotionally, spiritually, mentally, as well as physically.

Remember, your spouse is not just a tool in your life that you can use to make yourself better. He or she isn't just a "software program" you can throw into the computer of your life to complete the areas of your life that are incomplete. Your spouse is an expression of God's love for you, and as your love for each other grows and matures, it becomes a greater and greater expression of who God really is.

What kind of love am I talking about? You can find a description of it in First Corinthians 13:4-8 (*AMP*):

Love endures long and is patient and kind; love never is envious nor boils over with jealousy, is not boastful or vainglorious, does not display itself haughtily.

It is not conceited (arrogant and inflated with pride); it is not rude (unmannerly) and does not act unbecomingly. Love (God's love in us) does not insist on its own rights or its own way, for it is not self-seeking; it is not touchy or fretful or resentful; it takes no account of the evil done to it [it pays no attention to a suffered wrong].

It does not rejoice at injustice and unrighteousness, but rejoices when right and truth prevail.

Love bears under anything and everything that comes, is ever ready to believe the best of every person, its hopes are fadeless under all circumstances, and it endures everything [without weakening].

Love never fails [never fades out or becomes obsolete or comes to an end]....

This passage describes who God is, because God *is* love (1 John 4:16). Therefore, in order for you to be everything God wants you to be in your marriage, this passage describes what you must be to your spouse. You must endure long. You must be kind and not easily provoked. You must not seek your own way nor think evil of your spouse. And you must not behave rudely toward him or her.

That's *God's* perspective of what marriage should be. If you'd like to begin to experience that kind of marital bliss, read on!

Chapter 2

WHEN YOU FIND
THE TREASURE,
YOU BUY THE FIELD

One reason there are so many problems in so many marriages is that one or both partners are personally dysfunctional. They come into the marriage with emotional baggage from the past that, if not dealt with, can eventually sabotage the relationship.

"You treat me just like my father did!"

"Don't be my mother!"

"Don't tell me what to do! Just leave me alone!"

And the list goes on and on. However, the most common dysfunctional behavior in struggling marriages is *self-centeredness*.

One or both partners are focused only on themselves: *What's in this for me? What can I get out of this? How is my spouse going to meet my needs?*

You see, we live in a society that teaches us how to be dysfunctional. In order to be normal, we have to be *ab*normal. Just read a modern psychological periodical, and you'll see what I mean. What was once called *dysfunction* is now labeled a normal *function*. In fact, we are the first generation in which the dysfunctional are actually in the majority! (As for me, I just want to learn how to *function* in *conjunction* with the *unction* of God!)

When you tell people that you live a moral life, they want to know what's wrong with you. "You believe in God? You try to live according to the Bible? You're really weird!"

But do these people have a better alternative? They think they do — it's called *self*. But the truth is, their selfish flesh stinks just like everyone else's does. That's why we all need Jesus to make any area of our lives work — including our marriages!

So if you're in a dysfunctional marriage, don't feel alone. Many other marriage partners are experiencing the same kind of problems (1 Peter 5:9).

In Matthew 13:44, Jesus taught a parable that very aptly applies to the reality of an imperfect marriage. He talked about a treasure that a man found in a field. The man dug a hole and buried the treasure he had found. Then he went away, sold everything he had, and bought not just the *treasure*, but the *field*.

Now apply that parable to the subject of marriage. You see, my wife is no doubt convinced that I am inherently a great treasure. But the truth is, she didn't just get the treasure when she married me; she got the "field" too — all my personality traits, idiosyncrasies, and faults!

For instance, Linda has to put up with me eating chocolate M & M's. She likes to eat only healthy food, so she doesn't like chocolate. But I do — and I plan on living as long as she does! That's part of the field Linda bought when she got her treasure called Robb!

Wives, Submit to Your Husbands

First Peter 3:1-7 addresses couples who are in dysfunctional marriages, but the principles found in this passage apply to any marriage. The first two verses of this passage specifically address the wife:

> **Wives, likewise, be submissive to your own husbands, that even if some do not obey the word, they, without a word, may be won by the conduct of their wives,**
> **when they observe your chaste conduct accompanied by fear.**
>
> **1 Peter 3:1,2**

Perhaps you are a wife in a dysfunctional marriage and are having a difficult time submitting to your husband. Just remember — you still have Jesus to love and submit to. After all, when you submit to your husband, you're actually submitting to Jesus.

So many wives shake their fist at God and say, "I don't want to submit! I don't want to listen. I want to do what *I* want to do! Why does he get to do what he wants to do, and I don't?"

If you're a woman and still single, and you think that one day *you'll* probably feel that way about your husband, I strongly suggest that you don't get married. If you don't ever want to take instructions from your husband, then you really don't want to get married. Remember, in order to get the treasure, you have to buy the entire field, and no husband you ever get will be perfect.

However, don't think that men are free from having to take instructions themselves. If thou thinkest that, thou art very wrong! Men have to put up with instructions every day when they go to work. That's why they often come home and say, "My boss doesn't know anything! I'm telling you, if I owned the company..."

You see, it's the same thing all over again — no one's flesh likes to submit to his or her rightful authority! But no matter what realm of life we're talking about, anything with two heads is a freak!

Just imagine a bunch of Marines all standing in line at attention. Suddenly the captain walks by with a large array of bars and medals hanging all over his uniform, attesting to all he has accomplished during his military career. One of the privates leans over to the soldier next to him and whispers, "Why does he get to be captain? He shouldn't get to be captain. *I* want to be captain!"

That private should never have joined the Marines with that attitude! In the same way, if a woman wants to be the boss in her marriage, she shouldn't even get married. That just isn't the way God designed marriage to work.

God tells the wife, "Submit to your husband *as unto the Lord*" (Eph. 5:22). In other words, He is saying, "When you're submitting to your husband, you're actually submitting to *Me*."

And understand this: *Submission is a dormant word until agreement is no more.* Only when a wife disagrees with her husband does submission even come alive.

People often make the mistake of thinking that agreement and submission are synonymous. Therefore, they reason, marriage partners have to agree on an issue before making a decision.

But if I only make decisions in my marriage when my wife and I are in agreement, all I'm doing is playing an adult form of "Mother, May I?" I've gone from asking my mom, "Is it okay if I do this?" to asking my wife, "Do you feel that this is okay?"

A marriage relationship that cannot make a decision without agreement between the husband and wife is a dys-functional marriage. In a healthy marriage, there will be times when the husband has to exercise his authority as head of the home and make the final decision according to his best judgment, with or without his wife's agreement. These are the times the wife is commanded to submit to her husband *as unto the Lord*.

Of course, the opposite can be true as well. In other words, there are times when it may be best to wait on making the final decision. However, that is for the husband and not for the wife to say.

But what happens if the husband doesn't live up to the position of authority God has called him to hold in the marriage? What happens if he doesn't nurture his wife with the Word of God or protect her as Christ protects him?

The wife then begins to take authority over areas for which God has not made her responsible. Soon she has changed roles, becoming not only the nurturer, but the provider. This, too, is a sorry situation that creates a dysfunctional marriage.

'Zero to a Hundred' Or the Other Way Around?

Submission for my wife can't be easy, even though we have a great marriage. She thinks differently than I do on a lot of subjects. For instance, she is much more cautious about warming up to people than I am. She makes people qualify for a deeper relationship with her.

Many people make others qualify for their love, keeping their relationships in this "zero to a hundred" mode. In other words, a new person in their lives always starts at "zero." This new person then has to work up to "one hundred," the level that qualifies him or her for a close relationship with them.

On the whole, I don't consider this to be the best approach in a marriage relationship. There is merit in proving one's love for another, but not because the other partner demands it.

As for me, I qualified for Linda's love when she finally saw that no matter what she did, I would continue to love her. You see, we fell in love before we were Christians. After I got saved, Linda was having a problem with my new life as a Christian. She had stayed with me throughout the ordeal that landed me in a mental institution. But when I came out of that institution, I was a new creature in Christ, a Jesus person — and that was something she just didn't understand!

One night Linda was having a little tantrum about my new stand for Christ. She sat in her rocking chair, fiercely rocking back and forth as she poured out her frustration to me. "You may have been a little confused before," she declared, "but now you're out of your tree!"

I just walked over to her, put my arms around her, and said, "Linda, I love you. And it doesn't matter what you do, I will still keep loving you."

At that moment, the tide turned in our relationship. I guess I hit the "hundred" mark and qualified!

The problem with the "zero to a hundred" perspective is that people can live their entire lives in relationships they're never sure will work out. In contrast, I live my life according to the "hundred to zero" perspective. When someone new comes in my life, I'm ready to be 100% committed to that person. That person can do no wrong in my eyes. He is "preapproved," and I'll do anything in the world I can for him.

There is only one thing that could ever block the way of my 100% commitment to that relationship. Although I immediately accepted that person for who he is, he could disqualify *himself* by demonstrating that he is not who he said he is.

Of course, there is a way back to a close relationship if a person disqualifies himself. But now he has put himself on proving ground. He'll have to prove himself to me before I'll allow him back to the "hundred" mark in my life, where a position of trust and close relationship is regained.

How does the "hundred to zero" perspective work in my marriage? Well, as I told Linda long ago, I love her and accept her no matter what. She does not have to qualify for an inheritance. I don't have a prenuptial agreement with her. She doesn't have to prove anything to me. When I found this treasure, I willingly bought the "field"!

However, my wife *does* have to prove herself according to God's standard for her life. God has called me to be in her life what the Spirit of Christ is in my life. So I can help her by saying, "Honey, I don't want you to be anything different for me. I love you as you are. But I know you want to be everything God wants you to be, and I'm called to help you bring forth that potential in your life. Therefore, I'm not going to lie to you by encouraging behavior that hinders you from the very goal you desire."

How my wife and I approach relationships is only one area in which we see things differently. But through the years, we have come a long way in learning how to work through these differences of opinion according to God's Word. For Linda's part, she understands that God wants her to willingly submit to my leadership in the marriage, even when she disagrees with me. As she obeys God through submission, she knows she can trust Him to cause each situation to work out for the good.

Submission is not always easy for the wife, but it is what God requires. When the wife lovingly submits to her husband as unto the Lord, a crucial step is taken out of dysfunction into God's ordained order for marriage!

Husbands, Dwell With Your Wife With Understanding

Now I want to address myself to the husband. I never want anyone to get the idea that I don't deal with men regarding their attitudes and the situations they face inside their homes.

First Peter 3:7 says this: *"Husbands, likewise, dwell with them with understanding, giving honor to the wife, as to the weaker vessel, and as being heirs together of the grace of life, that your prayers may not be hindered."*

In other words, Peter is saying, "Husband, dwell with your wife with a conscious sensitivity." Think back to the time when you were courting your wife. You didn't have any problem giving honor unto her then, did you? I bet you opened doors for her and helped her put on her coat. You took her to the nicest restaurants. You pulled out her chair for her and then pushed it gently back under the table after she was seated. You said, "Hey, Sweetheart, is there any way I can make you more comfortable?"

41

I guarantee you, husband, you were something else! You were like a man from another world! And I bet you never looked like a slob when you were with her before you were married either. You fixed yourself up all the time; you made yourself look absolutely top notch — like F. W. Woolworth on the day he became a millionaire!

But now you've been married for a while, and you've become the biggest couch potato anyone has ever met! Actually, you're not even a couch potato anymore. You're a couch *watermelon*!

Sometimes when I see husbands and wives walking together, I think, *What's that guy doing, holding hands with his daughter like that?* Then I find out that the woman isn't his daughter at all — it's his wife! She just kept herself looking good over the years, and he let himself go!

I never want a day to come when my wife is ashamed of being married to me. You should be the same way. Never let the day come when your wife is ashamed that you are her husband. Maintain that line of respect between you and her by striving to be the best man you can be in every arena of life.

Peter said, *"Likewise, ye husbands, dwell with them* [your wives] *according to knowledge...."* (v. 7 *KJV*). You must endeavor to intimately get to know your wife so you can better understand her. But remember, any understanding you obtain about her has to be *learned*. You don't automatically have that understanding in you. It just isn't there.

Don't think that you know how your wife thinks. She will tell you, "You *think* you know how I think, but you *don't* know how I think!" I'm here to tell you, husband — she's right!

It's a foregone conclusion that you do not know how women think. Women think differently than men. Not only that, but they are also often smarter, more spiritual, and more sensitive than men.

While you sleep all the way through your kids having a problem in the middle of the night, your wife hears the first whimper. Besides taking care of the kids, she can handle every job at home that you don't want to do and therefore delegate to her. The truth is, your wife probably does more for the family than you do. That's why God says you must dwell with her according to knowledge and treat her with honor as the weaker vessel!

In Ephesians 5:25, the apostle Paul also addresses husbands, saying, *"Husbands, love your wives, just as Christ also loved the church and gave himself for her."* Now, giving yourself for your wife means that at times, you may have to endure something you don't understand without trying to fix it.

You see, men are problem solvers. That certainly describes me. If you don't want me to fix the problem, don't talk to me about it. It's too frustrating to hear about problems if you won't let me fix them!

But even though you're by nature a problem solver, you are to love your wife as Christ loved the Church. How does Christ love you? Well, He doesn't say to you, "I'm going to love you as soon as you get your attitude right." He also doesn't say, "I'll love you as soon as you submit to Me."

We've heard the question, "Which came first, the chicken or the egg?" Well, which comes first, submission or love? First John 4:19 tells us, *"We love Him because He first loved us."* In the same way, a wife will more willingly submit to a husband who first shows love to her as Christ loves the Church.

There may be times when your wife seems unlovable. But even then you must love her with openness. You may have a smile on your face, but she knows it when you're putting off a cold breeze behind that smile.

"What's wrong?" she asks.

"Nothing."

"Why aren't you as warm to me as you used to be?"

"I don't understand," you respond. "What did I do wrong? I don't get it."

All of a sudden, your wife is on a downward spiral of low self-esteem. I'm telling you, my friend, if you don't dwell with your wife according to knowledge and love her as Christ loved the Church, you will be trying to convince her that you love her throughout your entire married life!

Loving Your Wife
Means Giving to Your Wife

How do you love your wife as Christ loves the Church? Well, for one thing, you can't stop giving to someone you love with that kind of love. Just think for a moment about your relationship with your children. If you're a normal parent, you're always looking for a day when your children do something right so you can do something for them. You think, *Please, be good just for one day! Go into an emotional coma if you have to, because I just have to give you something!*

Well, Jesus is the same way. It's His nature to give abundant blessings to His Church. So if you are going to love your wife as Jesus loves the Church, you have to become a giver of good things to her!

Personally, I give flowers to my wife at least fifteen to twenty times a year. She also consistently receives gifts from me. If I'm traveling somewhere in the world, I usually spend quite a bit of money on her as I look for clothes or other items that would please her. Why am I always looking for a way to bless Linda through giving? Because my love for her drives me to give!

You may say, "But I can't love my wife like Christ loves the Church! That's too hard!" You're smart to realize that. It's impossible to love someone with that kind of love in your own human strength. But you *can* walk in this kind of love as you relate first to God and then to your wife.

You see, God expects every part of a marriage to be a reflection of the couple's relationship with *Him*, not with each other. The wife is to submit *as unto the Lord*. The husband is to love *as Christ loved the Church*. They are both to forgive one another, *even as God in Christ has forgiven them* (Eph. 4:32).

The truth is, when a married couple recognize the biblical perspective of marriage, they realize they are both under the hand of God and that there is really no first place and second place in their marriage relationship. Both have been given tasks to fulfill that are impossible in their own natural strength. Both must depend completely on divine grace and strength to fulfill their God-ordained roles in marriage. It takes faith to be a husband, and it takes faith to be a wife.

Give Your Wife What Is Due Her

In First Corinthians chapter 7, the apostle Paul takes another turn in dealing with issues regarding marriage. He discusses what to do in an unequally yoked marriage between a believer and an unbeliever (vv. 12-16). He also gives some scriptural insight regarding fixed marriages (vv. 36-38).

As an aside, I'm convinced of the fact that fixed marriages often work better than "picked" marriages in which two people choose each other as their marriage partners. Why is that? Because in a fixed marriage, the husband and wife enter the union knowing in advance what responsibilities they each must fulfill.

But when people pick their marriage partner, they try to find someone who will fulfill some of *their* responsibilities so they don't have to! That's often what causes fights in marriages. One or both marriage partners are either falling short of their own responsibilities in marriage, or they want the other partner to fulfill needs that only God can fulfill.

In First Corinthians 7:3 (*KJV*), it says, *"Let the husband RENDER unto the wife due benevolence: and likewise also the wife unto the husband."* The word "render" here means *to give*. So Paul is saying, "Let the husband *give* unto the wife due benevolence...."

The word "due" refers to a debt that cannot be repaid — a debt that is owed to God. Paul is saying, "Let the husband give with a good attitude the debt he owes to

God, which can never be stamped 'Paid in Full.'" The word "benevolence" actually carries the meaning of *thinking good thoughts*. Putting all this together, you could paraphrase this verse, "Let the husband give unto the wife according to the debt that can never be repaid to God, thinking grace thoughts about her and giving her the affection that is due her."

Let the husband give. It's a choice, husband. In your marriage and in my marriage, it is a choice.

The hard reality is that life is not kind to romance. In fact, at times the daily routine of life can seem to be the greatest enemy of romance. And as the years go by, a husband can tend to make his wife a tool he uses without even providing proper care. If the wife allows that situation to continue, she becomes someone she was never meant to become.

In this kind of situation, the couple eventually comes to a place in their marriage where no understanding exists between them any longer. And it all started because the husband failed to give his wife the care and affection that was due her.

I know from experience what I'm talking about. For 23 hours and 59 minutes every day, I have to be an understanding giver of mercy. Every day I have to listen with understanding to people's problems. I may want to kick some of them in the seat of the pants and say, "I can't believe you're talking to me about this! I've been preaching to you for five years, and you act like you've gotten nothing out of it!" But I don't say that. Instead, I say, "Oh, that's okay. You're going to be all right. Let's just pray together. I really believe that God is going to touch you."

I'm like that for every person in the world — except for Linda. Too often she is the one who catches that one minute out of every 24 hours when I'm not feeling very understanding. And she can't figure out why I'm one way with everyone else and another way with her.

Once I told her in frustration, "Well, you hear my preaching all the time. You ought to know it all by now. But when are you ever going to get around to doing it?"

I never should have said that to my wife. I expected something out of her that I don't expect out of any other person in life. I didn't give to her due benevolence. I didn't dwell with her according to knowledge. I'm like every other man on this earth. I still have a lot to learn about how to treat my wife with the understanding and affection that is due her!

But Linda keeps on believing in me, even when I mess up. She knows that when she found her treasure, she also bought the field! And it helps to know that each day, we are both working at taking a few more "rocks" out of our fields that hinder us from growing closer in our marriage relationship. We're both determined to make our marriage the best it can possibly be.

Catch that same vision for your marriage. You found a precious treasure when you found your spouse. So cherish the treasure, and accept the field that came with it. In the meantime, throw out any "rocks" that clutter your own field. Don't let anything hinder you from becoming the husband or wife God has called you to be!

Chapter 3

FIVE BASIC NEEDS
OF THE
HUSBAND AND WIFE

Programmed into the spirits of men and women are certain personal needs that are unique to each gender. When these needs are realized and acted upon in a marriage, that marriage begins to become what God designed it to be.

Some people think that if they renew their minds with God's Word, they'll reach a place in their spiritual walk where they don't have these needs any longer. But underneath it all remains the deep desire to be clothed with that which the first man and woman was clothed before they fell. Underneath it all, these basic needs lie hidden, waiting to be fulfilled.

I want to give you five basic corresponding needs of both women and men. You and your spouse should make it your personal quest to meet these needs for each other more than you ever have before. As you do, your home will be transformed forever!

#1 Need of the Wife: Affection

The first thing the wife needs is *affection* without sex. Husband, you've been taking from her since the day you met her. Learn how to give into her life. She needs you to put your arm around her, even when you don't want anything from her. She needs you to hold her hand even when you're not looking for anything else. She needs you to nudge her over closer to you when you're sitting together on the couch or church pew.

Show your wife that she's as important to you as she was when you first got married. Show her that you care for her now as much as you ever did. She needs to be held. She needs to be loved. She needs to be cared for. She needs to be given the security of closeness and intimacy without sex.

I know that's a difficult challenge for us as husbands because we're geared in one direction — the physical act of sex. We don't think the way our wives do. But if we fail to show our wives the affection they need, we'll sabotage our sexual relationship with them. They'll start telling us, "The only thing you ever want is sex!"

Let me say this to you, husband: Your wife is not a legal prostitute for you, and affection isn't just the prelude to a sexual encounter. Lovemaking doesn't start when you go to bed at night. Lovemaking starts with a consistent demonstration of affection that begins when you open your eyes in the morning.

Find ways throughout the day to show affection to your wife through a gentle touch or a loving word. Tell her that your desire is to be with her. Tell her how much she means to you. Tell her that you're excited to go out every day and be a winner so you can bring home to her what you produce with the work of your hands.

Tell her how much she excites and pleases you.

That's how you create a desire in your wife to come near to you. That's how you kindle a flame in her that never burns out!

#1 Need of the Husband: Sexual Fulfillment

Whereas the first need of the wife is for affection, the first thing the husband needs is *sexual fulfillment*. If you're a wife, you've probably already figured that out!

But don't just lightly pass off your husband's desire for sex. It's a very real need, and if you don't give him the sexual fulfillment he needs and desires, you leave the door open for someone else to come in and do it!

As the wife, you must realize that you're the one who sets the sexual temperature in your home. If you don't have a good attitude about making love to your husband, your husband won't come anywhere near you. Or even if he does, he'll come and get what he wants without considering what you need at all — that is, unless he is doing very, very well at believing and acting on the Word!

You see, most men are considerate in this sense: They will not continually push themselves on someone who doesn't want them. A husband will allow his wife to go her own way. If she shows no interest, she will receive no interest from him. Soon their relationship will begin to draw apart.

Suddenly a young woman down at the office offers a listening ear to the frustrated husband. The devil whispers to the husband, *What about her? She's understanding. She's loving. She's everything your wife isn't.* The husband begins to share some of his sexual frustrations with his lovely coworker, and the door is opened for adultery and a ruined marriage.

So learn how to fulfill your husband sexually as much as possible. Work on becoming physically exciting to him.

Let Proverbs 31:17 be your guide: *"She girds herself with strength, and strengthens her arms."* Strengthen your desire for your husband throughout the day by thinking about making love to him. Mentally and emotionally prepare yourself for that sexual encounter. Think about how you can hardly wait for him to come home. Think about how you want to please him, to love him, to be with him. Keep him from ever looking for excitement anywhere else!

#2 Need of the Wife: Conversation

The second thing a wife needs is *conversation*. Personally, I'm not a very good conversationalist. Sometimes I have to force myself to hold a conversation with people. So when I get home, I think I've already said it all and Linda already knows it all!

But no matter how much you've talked to other people at work during the day, your wife needs you to converse with *her*. And that doesn't mean you just allow your eardrums to vibrate as you *hear* her talk.

It means you actually *listen* to her. She needs to know her perspective has worth to you. You don't reject or disqualify her feelings. You value what she says.

Now, this isn't always easy for men to do. Listening is a skill that usually doesn't come naturally to a man. He has to make the commitment to learn how to listen carefully to his wife's words in order to better understand her heart.

Personally, I find it difficult when I listen to my wife's thoughts on a particular issue and then have to make a decision contrary to her perspective. I truly value Linda's input, and I want to consider her feelings. But at the same time, I have to do what I believe God wants me to do. God has made *me* responsible for that decision, not Linda. I don't want to get caught in the trap of becoming someone I'm not for her or for anyone else at the expense of obeying God.

In this type of situation, the wife may say, "My husband never lets me talk to him about anything. He just does what he wants to do and doesn't listen to anyone."

Many husbands have to plead guilty to that accusation. But what if the husband is truly endeavoring to listen to his wife before he makes a decision he believes is best for the family? In that case, after everything has been said and all the conversation is over, it is the wife's responsibility to support her husband rather than to sit back and silently curse his decision.

That's what submission is all about. It requires first an interior adjustment, a conscious choice to submit. That then leads to an exterior agreement: "All right, family, we're going to get behind Dad's decision because he believes it's the right thing to do."

When a wife willingly submits in this type of situation, it demonstrates to the husband that she loves and reverences him. He can rest assured that she has his best interests at heart. This makes it much easier for him to converse with her about important or sensitive issues in the future because he isn't thinking, *She's just waiting for me to fail.*

#2 Need of the Husband: Companionship

The wife's need for conversation corresponds with the husband's need for *companionship*. He needs his wife to be with him. He needs her to *want* to do things with him that he enjoys.

As for me, I don't like traveling without Linda. Of course, I realize there will be times when she just can't go along with me. But I like it very much when she can!

What is a husband looking for in the arena of companionship? Well, first let me tell you what he *isn't* looking for. He doesn't need a cook. He doesn't need a second mother. He also doesn't need a conscience. He doesn't even need a sexual partner. He can buy that without all the baggage and responsibility. That's not what he's looking for.

The husband is looking for someone to walk with him through the situations of life. He's looking for someone to believe in him. He's looking for someone for whom he can be a champion.

You see, once a man receives the revelation of how to stop being self-centered, he has a tremendous need to give to someone who will receive. However, because of low self-esteem, most women don't know how to receive and be thankful for what is given. Therefore, they respond with suspicion, saying things like, "Why are you doing this? Are you trying to buy me?"

If the wife continues to negatively respond to her husband's giving to her, her persistence will shut him down. It's very difficult for a man to be as persistent as a woman in a relationship. His energies have to be focused on all the challenges he faces every day in providing for the family. She's being protected from a lot of the things he confronts on a daily basis, so her energies can be more focused on him. Unfortunately, the wife often focuses on what she sees *wrong* in her husband's life, when she's supposed to be focused on what's *right* with him!

A husband doesn't need someone who can't look past his faults and highly esteem his worth as a man. He needs someone who walks through life with him thinking, *This man I married is so great! I couldn't have married a better man!*

Someone once asked Ruth Graham, wife of evangelist Billy Graham, in an interview, "Doesn't it bother you that Billy is gone as much as he is? Doesn't that really hurt your home life." At the time the interviewer asked her this question, Billy was gone at least six to eight months out of the year conducting evangelistic crusades.

Ruth replied, *"I would rather have a slice of a great man than the whole of a common man."*

Also, my wife Linda once asked a great woman of God named Robina Daniels, "What do you want most in life?" (Robina Daniels is the wife of Peter Daniels, the single greatest spiritual influence in my life.)

Robina replied, *"To be everything Peter wants me to be."*

Contained within these two women's answers lies the key to a woman's success in a marriage. She places importance on what is important to her husband. Her lifetime goal is to be pleasing to him.

A wife who fulfills her role as a loving, loyal companion is a priceless treasure to her husband. Do you know why? Because people will pretend they want to please him every second of the day for money. They'll tell him what a great guy he is for a few bucks. But what he really wants is someone who esteems him and wants to please him just because of her love for him.

Why would I ever want a secretary or some other woman to fulfill my need for companionship? That woman would only be doing it because she doesn't know me. But I have a woman at home who knows me intimately and *still* remains my most loyal supporter and steadfast companion!

You know, women look at me and marvel, "Oh, he's just so wonderful. He must be such a great husband!"

I tell them, "You know what? You couldn't handle me! You'd think I was on your case every day — making sure you set the correct atmosphere in my life with your appearance and your demeanor so you could help me fulfill what I'm called to do. You couldn't take living with me — but Linda can! She's just the companion I need!"

That's how every husband should feel about his wife!

#3 Need of the Wife: Honesty and Transparency

The third thing the wife needs is *honesty and openness*. She needs her husband to be honest and open in his dealings with her.

You may say, "Well, that's it! I'm going to tell her the sin I've been in for ten years!" No, don't just jump in and make a mess of things! You need to start with the smaller issues and let your openness grow from there. But understand this, husband: *Your wife wants to know you.* Therefore, she needs you to immediately begin to work toward becoming more open and honest with her than you've ever been before.

I speak to so many women who have no idea what their husbands are really like. These wives have no clue about how much money is in their bank accounts because their husbands keep them away from all the family business.

I recently ministered to a woman who had been doing very well in business before she got married a few years ago. Now they are $300,000 in unsecured debt, and she doesn't even know how it happened! There is no transparency or openness in that marriage. The husband hasn't matched with actions the words he has spoken to his wife.

You see, the truth is not in what a person says. The truth is also not necessarily in what a person does. The truth lies where these two lines of saying and doing converge. In other words, there may be valid reasons why a person had to do what he did; in that case, his past actions may not represent him well. Or there may be understandable reasons why a person said what he did, even though what he said wasn't right.

That's what I mean when I say that often the truth actually lies where these two lines of saying and doing meet. Therefore, the only way two marriage partners can discern the truth in their relationship is for both of them to be open and honest with each other regarding both their words and their actions.

Here's an important point for the woman to consider, however: Although she needs truth and openness from her husband, at the same time she must be *ready* for truth. That's where the third need of the husband comes into play.

#3 Need of the Husband: Acceptance and Approval

On the backside of the wife's need for the husband to be honest and open with her is the husband's need for his wife's *acceptance and approval* whenever he *is* honest and open.

A wife needs to accept her husband's honesty without trying to use what he has told her to control him or manipulate him into doing something she wants him to do.

A wife can do this by refusing to show unconditional acceptance of her husband when he is honest with her. Her disapproval of him begins to work on him little by little until eventually the husband yields and the wife gets her way. But that's a sure way to keep the husband from ever being honest and open again!

Another reason why some husbands aren't open with their wives is that their wives jump down their throat every time they do try to be open. Contrary to popular opinion, most men don't like to argue. That's not how they normally resolve conflict.

If two men get angry with each other, they may say, "Shut your mouth or I'll punch you!" But once they blow off steam, the conflict is over. They'll put their arms around each other and go out for lunch together.

On the other hand, women usually want to talk and talk and talk to resolve a conflict. And even when the argument is over, for the woman it isn't over. So the husband is often reluctant to be honest and open with his wife because he doesn't want to raise questions in her mind that will start an argument. He knows there will be thirty more questions he can't answer after he tells her the truth.

So what would the best way be for the wife to respond when her husband is being open and honest with her? She should just listen and be understanding. Proverbs 19:14 (*TLB*) says, "*A father can give his sons homes and riches, but only the Lord can give them understanding wives.*"

An understanding wife is a gift from the Lord because she will attempt to do everything she can in order to see things from her husband's perspective. She will also bide her time, waiting for the right time to approach him with questions she has regarding a sensitive subject.

Esther is an example of this type of wife. She waited for the right time to approach her husband, the king, with a sensitive request (Esther 4:15-7:10). Ruth is also a good example of a woman who knew how to wait for the proper timing to

present her request to her future husband, Boaz (Ruth 3:1-11).

Wife, there is a time to approach your
husband, and there is a time not to
approach him. There's a time when you
can ask him anything, and he'll say yes.
And there is a time when you can ask him
the smallest, simplest thing — something
you're sure will receive a positive
response, but you're just asking him to be
nice — and he'll say, "No."

So learn the timings of your husband.
Become an understanding wife, and give
your husband the acceptance and
approval he needs as he endeavors to
open his heart to you. That will start a
process that leads to an intimacy with
your husband you've only dreamed about
before!

#4 Need of the Wife:
Financial Security

Husband, the fourth thing your wife
needs is *financial security*. She should
never have to think, *Oh, my Lord, what
are we going to do? We have all these bills!*

How are we going to pay them? Don't put her underneath the burden of those bills. Don't make her think she has to go get a job so they can get paid.

Let me tell you something, husband. Your wife should never *have* to work. What she does at home is more than what you do at the workplace. I mean, you might go sit on the forklift all day long, but she's at home lifting all the little bambinos you gave her! She's changing diapers you don't want to change. She's going to the PTA meeting you want nothing to do with. Then you come home and ask her, "Well, what have you been doing all day? You don't have anything to do! You're just on marital welfare" — as if you were God's gift to making money!

Husband, you need to make it your aim to keep your wife feeling financially secure. "But I don't make enough money," you may say. Well, then, do one of two things. Change jobs, or lower your lifestyle until you do make more money!

What benefit is there in owning a bigger house if you're never there to enjoy it because you're always working? What benefit is there in owning a lot of material possessions if your wife has to work outside the home against her own wishes?

When you and your spouse are both working so hard that you hardly ever see each other, you open yourself up to temptation. And if divorce is the result, your pursuit of material gain just gives you more things to split up between the two of you!

Personally, I believe that when the children are small, a wife should not work outside the home. If anything, she can work at home in her free time to make a little extra income. That's why home-based businesses are becoming very big now — because mothers want to spend time with their children.

Once the children are well into high school or out on their own, that's the time for the wife to think about going back to work or becoming more involved in volunteer work for her church or for a charitable organization. For instance, she could visit the sick or go to rest homes and visit the elderly. She could also get involved in prison ministry and visit the prisons.

If the couple decides at that time that they want to buy a new home, a new car, or other extras, the wife can also go back to work to make sure they stay out of debt as they enjoy this season of their lives. Nevertheless, the husband remains the one who is primarily responsible for bringing in the family income.

I believe the notion that the wife can just as easily be the primary breadwinner is one the travesties of the modern age. But I can tell you how that notion began to gain acceptance in today's society. It started with the big push to make husbands and wives equal in the decision-making process within a marriage.

Husbands began to say, "Well, if you're going to be equal in the decision-making process, then you're going to be equal in the money-making process too." Then wives began to say, "If I'm going to be responsible for making money, you're not going to make the decisions about how I spend it."

That's when married couples started using two checkbooks. And now I'm hearing this from couples more and more: "Well, he pays the rent and the utilities, and I pay for all the other family expenses." I ask them, "How can you two call yourselves married?" Many modern couples have created such a separated existence, they've almost reached a state of legalized living together!

Christians need to leave behind all these worldly ideas about marriage and get back to *God's* way of doing things. Within the divine design for the covenant of marriage, God has built within the woman the need for financial security. That isn't a need the wife should have to struggle to fulfill herself. Rather, it is both the husband's responsibility and his privilege to provide for his family through the work of his own hands.

#4 Need of the Husband: Domestic Support

Next, let's talk about the husband's need for *domestic support*. This has to do with keeping the house clean, making sure his clothes are clean and pressed, and so on.

I get reports from husbands all the time whose wives lie around all day and never do anything to keep up the home. However, the husbands can't say anything about it to their wives because when they do, the wives make them pay for it dearly!

I've been in the homes of some very well-known ministers where the husband is looking all over the house for a sock or the wife casually says, "Oops! I forgot to iron your shirt." I sit there and think, *You need to live what you preach!*

You see, I'm called by God to raise the standard of my surroundings to the level at which I preach. My surroundings are that way. My house is always clean. We don't live with things strewn all over the place.

For the most part, my wife takes care of our home all by herself — and we have a pretty large home! I cannot understand wives who stay home all day, yet think they have to hire a housekeeper and a nanny for their three children!

Of course, I understand that each family's situation is different. You just have to deal with whatever is on your plate the best way you know how.

For instance, if a wife is working long hours either in a home-based business or outside the home, she will need help from the husband and children in keeping the house clean. Even if she's an at-home mother, the husband can still pitch in and help at times. He can tell the children, "Mommy wants to do this for you, but I wouldn't let her. I'm going to do it today just because I want to be with you." Whatever the situation is in your home, just stay positive so the children keep a healthy attitude about helping around the house and about marriage in general.

Personally, I help around the house all the time. You see, I spend much of my time at home, whereas Linda spends a lot of time at the office. I've found that if I go to the office, I don't get a lot accomplished because people always come to me, asking for a little of my time.

So when I need to spend time studying and praying, I usually do it at home. And while I walk around praying in the Spirit, I straighten up the house. It isn't that Linda expects me to do that. I do it because I *want* to.

Also, Linda gets up before me, so I'm the one who makes the bed. Every morning without fail, my bed is made within thirty seconds of the time I get out of bed. I help keep the rest of the bedroom clean too. The door to our bedroom stays open, and it always looks like something out of a home interior magazine!

The wife also provides domestic support to the husband by making sure the children understand that Daddy is the boss.

Wife, don't think I'm kidding for a minute. You need to make your children feel like their dad is just about an eighth of an inch lower than Jesus. Why? Because too often the demands of work keep husbands from enjoying much fellowship with their families as they watch their kids grow up.

That's why one of the greatest things you can ever do to meet your husband's need of domestic support is to build up his image in the children's eyes. You see, your children will believe about your husband whatever you tell them. He doesn't have as much opportunity to speak to them as you do, so it's up to you to help them get acquainted with their dad's admirable qualities.

When the children think of their dad, they should think, *My dad loves me. My dad's out making money so we can have a nice house. My dad loved me so much, he let me go to this school.* These are the kind of things you should be teaching your kids about their father!

But what will happen if you walk around complaining about your husband all the time? What if you often argue with him in front of the children? What if you're always taking the children's side when they disagree with their dad's decisions?

In that case, there will probably be a breakdown in your children's understanding of a healthy marriage relationship. They will grow up to one day challenge their own spouses, and they will sow their own disappointments into the hearts of their children.

So if you ever have a problem with your husband, *don't* deal with it in front of your kids, and *don't* talk to them about it. Your children are not your counselors!

I have a friend whose mother always told the children, "When Dad comes home, I want the home to be quiet and peaceful, and you should have all your homework done." This mother provided the domestic support her husband needed. She consistently built into her children an image of their dad that generated a deep sense of respect and love for him.

To this day, every one of the children in that family has grown up to be successful in his or her chosen field. That's the mark of a good wife!

#5 Need of the Wife: Family Commitment

The last need of the wife we're going to talk about is *family commitment*. Your wife needs to spend time with her family — her parents, her siblings, etc. Now, why she needs it, I don't really understand. It's a need most men don't have.

You know, you'll hardly ever find a female hermit. All the hermits of this world are men! When women get together, they all hug and talk, talk, *talk*. When they get together with family members, they hug when they get there; they hug while they're there; and they hug when they leave! And while the wife fellowships all day long, the husband falls asleep from boredom!

He says to her, "Hey, can we go yet? Come on, let's go!"

She replies, "Oh, come on, just a little while longer."

The kids plead, "Oh, Dad, let us stay! Please let's stay a little longer!"

And the husband thinks, *My Lord, all I've been doing here is sleeping or watching sports on television all day long!*

Men just don't have that same deep need for family commitment that women do. Men can go in their own house and just stay happily by themselves. Every once in a while, they might look out the window to make sure no one is coming down their block to visit. Their longstanding motto is "My house is my castle!"

But women are different than men (not better or worse — just different!). They love to visit their loved ones and fellowship with them. They love to play games together.

So the wife might say to the husband, "You never want to do anything with the family."

The husband thinks to himself, *I don't know what to do!* So he says to his wife, "Let's do what *you* want to do."

"Well, I don't want to do what I want to do. I want to do what *you* want to do."

The husband thinks, *But I don't want to do anything!*

I've certainly lived through similar scenarios in times past. Let me tell you something about myself: In the areas of my life for which I'm responsible, don't get in my way; I know what to do. But in areas I *don't* know about, such as planning family time, I'll just admit, "I don't know anything about this. It isn't that I don't want to have anything to do with it; it's just that I don't know. I'm not that smart!"

I don't think about playing Scrabble with the in-laws or about playing Monopoly with the kids. I think about, *Man, we need another bedroom!* I think about, *Hey, does she realize how much she spent on her charge card this month?* Those are the areas I'm responsible for, so that's what I think about! Nevertheless, I do understand that my wife needs time with her siblings and with her mother and father, so I try to make sure she has that time.

What if the wife's family lives out of state? Then the husband needs to provide enough income for her to spend at least a few days a year with her family. Now, of course, the husband also needs to honor *his* parents, but he doesn't have that same need to spend a lot of time with them.

You see, the man chose to move, but the woman was pulled away from her family. She gave up her name. Therefore, she needs time to return to the family she loves for a visit. The children also need a sense of heritage and relationship with their extended family — something the mother is usually best able to provide.

#5 Need of the Husband: Respect

The final need of the husband we'll discuss is perhaps his greatest need: A man needs to be *respected*.

When I walk in my house, I don't want to be immediately told, "Oh, hey, the garbage is over there. You need to take it out and dump it. Oh, and by the way, the bills are on the counter."

You know, that's the kind of greeting far too many men get when they come home from work. Life goes from morning till night without any celebration of Dad. There is nothing said about "Isn't Dad great? or "Aren't we thankful for how hard he works?" Instead of saying, "Let's pray for Daddy right now. He has to work late tonight," Mom says, "Dad is working late *again*."

It's the truth. The husband needs to be respected. Ephesians 5:33 says, *"...let the wife see that she respects her husband."* You may say, "Well, respect has to be earned." But notice this verse *doesn't* say, "Let the wife see that she respects her husband *when he deserves that respect."*

I believe it's true that in order for a husband to be respected, it helps greatly if he acts respectable. But if he doesn't, that doesn't change God's command to the wife to respect the husband.

As my wife, Linda needs to respect me. She doesn't only respect me when I'm acting respectable. She respects me because God has told her to respect me.

The truth is, respect isn't created when the receiver fulfills certain requirements. Respect is derived from the grace of the giver. For instance, even if a person hasn't acted respectable and has wrecked his life, I can still treat him with respect. I know there is some good thing in that person's life for which he was never recognized, and for that I can respect him.

So, wife, don't let a day go by without demonstrating your respect to your husband. If you're not careful, you'll start letting your reverence and respect for your husband slip. A day will turn into a week; a week will turn into a month; a month will turn into a cold, hard year, and your husband will still be waiting for the woman God gave him to fill his need for respect and appreciation.

It's Always Our Choice

We've looked at five of the basic needs of men and women that marriage partners are called to fulfill for each other. But let me ask you this: What do we do if our spouse isn't meeting our needs? Does that release us from our responsibility to meet our partner's needs?

No, it does not. You see, it's true that all these needs are very real. But when we put them all aside, the Word of God still tells those of us who are husbands to love our wives as Christ loved the Church. It still tells wives to submit to their husbands as unto the Lord.

Whether or not we meet our spouse's needs is always our choice. For instance, I could be like so many other husbands and say, "Well, I love my wife. But, you know, there are times when I just don't know if I have any more to give."

However, I choose not to have that attitude. I just stay submitted to the Word until I see that spark in my wife again, that desire to be the piece that fits into the hole of my heart. That gives me the drive to go at it all over again! I can love her, and she can submit to me. Little by little, our relationship continues to grow closer.

So what about your marriage? Are you and your spouse willing to fulfill each other's needs? Do you both want to build your marriage relationship according to the wisdom and the ways of God?

The answers to these questions will determine whether your marriage becomes a fading glory headed for disappointment and stagnation — or a light that shines ever brighter unto the perfect day!

PRAYER FOR YOUR MARRIAGE

If you want to live in your marriage *God's* way instead of the world's way, pray this prayer:

Father, I'm coming to You in the Name of Jesus. I am asking You to soften my heart toward my spouse. Cause me to only respond to You as I relate to her [or him]. I choose to make a quality decision never to take authority over something You haven't given me the responsibility of. I roll the whole of my care regarding my marriage on You because You care for me [1 Peter 5:7]. I thank You for working Your perfect will in both me and my spouse in Jesus' Name, amen.

FOR FURTHER INFORMATION

For additional copies of this book,
for further information regarding
Robb Thompson's ministry schedule,
or for a complete listing of
Robb Thompson's books, audiotapes,
and videotapes, please write or call:

Family Harvest Church
18500 92nd Ave.
Tinley Park, IL 60477
1-877-WIN-LIFE
(1-877-946-5433)

ABOUT THE AUTHOR

For more than a decade, Robb Thompson has pastored the congregation of Family Harvest Church in Tinley Park, Illinois, reaching out to the Chicago area with a practical, easily understood message of hope. A hallmark of his exciting ministry has been his ability to teach Christians how to act on God's Word and move out in faith so they can become *winners* in this life. Today, Robb Thompson's teaching ministry continues to grow through books, tapes, and the ever-expanding television program, *Winning in Life*, as he ministers to people throughout the United States and around the world.